LIGHT IN
THE DARKNESS

Happy are those who love God.... They are a light in the darkness for the upright.

LIGHT IN THE DARKNESS

New Reflections on the Psalms
for Every Day
of the Year

JOAN D. CHITTISTER, OSB

A Crossroad Book
The Crossroad Publishing Company
New York

Translations of passages from the Psalms are taken from *Five-Week Psalter (Inclusive Language)*, copyright © 1985 Benedictine Sisters of Erie, Inc., 6101 East Lake Road, Erie, PA 16511.

The Crossroad Publishing Company
370 Lexington Avenue, New York, NY 10017

Copyright © 1998 by Joan D. Chittister, OSB

Title page art by Jeffry A. Braun

Printed in the United States of America

Library of Congress Cataloging-in-Publication Data

Chittister, Joan.
    Light in the darkness : new reflections on the Psalms for every day of the year / Joan Chittister.
       p. cm.
    ISBN 0-8245-1748-2 (pbk.)
    1. Bible. O.T. Psalms – Meditations. 2. Devotional calendars.
I. Title.
BS1430.4.C475   1998
242'.2 – dc21   97-52355

1 2 3 4 5 6 7 8 9 10   02 01 00 99 98

This book is dedicated to
Mary Luke Tobin, SL,
and
Barbara Thomas, SCN,
women who have been
light in the darkness to many
— especially to me.

INTRODUCTION

The psalms are the oldest prayers in the Judeo-Christian tradition. There are 150 of them, and, like hymns today, they were written for multiple occasions. They are a lexicon of the human condition. They trace the human condition back thousands of years. They assure us that our own hopes and fears, desires and emotions are shared by the rest of humankind. Say this month's verse from the psalms before every reading. By the end of the month, say it from memory. It will find a soft spot in your heart. Most of all, it will bring your heart the comfort of the ages.

JANUARY

Psalm 16

*You will show me
the path of life,
the fullness of joy
in your presence.*

*T*he path of life is a sinuous system. We want it to be straight and clear. It very seldom is. It unfolds a little at a time while we're living it. We talk about "planning it" and "finding it," but it is much more often discovered in hindsight than in vision. More often than not, we do not find it; it finds us. The only question is whether we recognize it and accept it when it comes, whether we bring meaning to it and take meaning from it as it is.

Psychologists talk a great deal these days about "alienation," that feeling of being out of touch with the self, of not knowing exactly what we're about in life or how we feel about it or what things mean to us as we race always from one place to the next looking for what we want but cannot identify. Social analysts say that alienation began to mark us as a people when the assembly line began to take the place of craft. People bolted steel frames or sorted peaches or cut pants pockets all their lives but never felt the exhilarating sense of creativity that comes with building a car, or growing an orchard, or designing a suit of clothes. We became specialists. We got removed from the whole to concentrate on the parts of life. Doctors studied the liver, not the person; lawyers concentrated on property law, not jurisprudence; researchers experimented on one gene, not the genetic system. We worked — hard and with intensity — but too often without a sense of the sum or a feeling of conscious accomplishment. Meaning, in a world like that, needs to be found somewhere else. The results of assembly-line disorientation are not all bad, however. They force us back on things other than on what we do for a living to justify our existence, to explain our purpose in life.

Clearly, it all comes down to finding "the fullness of joy in God's presence." Maybe alienation is the sign that we are not a secular culture after all. Maybe, in fact, we are a very spiritual one suffering because we have been cast adrift, separated from all the props and left to find for ourselves the things that really count in life.

January 1: New Year's resolutions are a waste of time. What we may really need are New Year's questions — those issues that we intend this year to study, read about, and discuss with others so that our hearts may be broken open and our souls engaged in the real business of life.

January 2: You can always tell people who have lost a sense of the meaning of life: they emphasize only one dimension of it. They wear themselves out on clothes or people or sports or work or even prayer and wonder why life feels so empty.

January 3: Meaning does not come from what we do. It comes from what we are. If we are lovers of beauty, then beauty will fill us all our days. If we are committed to justice, then justice will drive us past all fatigue or failure. If we are devoted to building human community, then we will find meaning in the people whose lives we touch. It's when we are driven by nothing other than our daily schedules that life becomes gray, listless, and dour.

January 4: To be indifferent to the world around us, to absent ourselves from its struggles, to ignore our responsibility to shape it, to wait for things to happen around us rather than to enable them to happen within us is to be out of touch with life. It is a sad and empty existence.

January 5: Life happens quickly but the meaning of it comes into focus only slowly, slowly, slowly. The challenge is to keep on asking ourselves what it is.

January 6: Achievement is what we do for ourselves. Meaning comes out of what we do for others.

January 7: Beware the day you feel no feelings. It is a sign of spiritual sclerosis, of internal death.

January 8: Too often we treat feelings as a demonstration of emotional weakness rather than a sign of emotional health. Sometimes the only appropriate response to life is to feel bad about it. At other times, to be "objective" about things that deserve unadulterated feeling is the greatest sin.

January 9: Struggle is a commitment to life. It's when we stop struggling for something that we have lost the ability to be human.

January 10: Argumentation never leads to change. Only feeling can either initiate or sustain the long, hard journey to new life. What we do not feel for, we will not commit ourselves to die for.

January 11: Alienation — that feeling of disinterest and distance from concern — is a dry, cold sterility of soul that leaves us breathing but dead of heart.

January 12: When we cease to monitor our feelings, we sink into a cotton batten of life, a charade of humanity that fears to be honest about things for fear of what it would cost us to face them.

January 13: When we don't care what we do, why we're doing it, or what will happen to it once it's done, that is alienation. It is a state of unholy robotization that rends soul and body.

January 14: Littering is a sign of alienation from the earth. National chauvinism in a global world is a sign of alienation from humankind. Addiction is a sign of alienation from the self. No wonder society is out of kilter.

January 15: To find meaning in life it is essential to ask always, "Why am I doing what I am doing? Who will profit from it? Who will be disadvantaged by it? What am I doing to make it better?"

January 16: Martina Navratilova said to a reporter once, "The moment of victory is much too short to live for that and nothing else." The implication is clear: to focus all of life on one dimension of it is to court emotional disaster.

January 17: When the work I do has more to do with survival than with commitment, it is imperative to commit myself to something more. I find that I have gone through life committed to absolutely nothing at all.

January 18: Not to know how we feel about a thing is to prostitute the soul to the mind, a dimension of humanity that is only one way of knowing and a weak one at best.

January 19: The important thing in life is not what we do. What matters is why we do it and how we feel about it. To be alienated is to have no answer to those questions.

January 20: The purpose of a sense of meaninglessness is to give us a taste for what is missing in us. Otherwise, we could be fooled into thinking that despite having nothing of value we had everything important in life.

January 21: When the emotions die, hope dies. Then there is no reason for change, no energy for change, no desire for change. Then the bad is good enough and we never come to the fullness of humanity that we are all meant to cultivate.

January 22: Life loses meaning when peoples are denied the right and the possibility of changing it.

January 23: "But what did you gain by becoming an American citizen?" the baffled Brit asked his friend. "Well, to begin with," the expatriot Englishman answered, "I just won the Revolutionary War." Point: life depends on the perspective from which we view it. Meaning does not reside in the thing itself. The meaning a thing has for us depends on the meaning we give it.

January 24: I am most alive when I am involved in making life for the world tomorrow better than it was yesterday. "Indifference," Ouida wrote, "is the invisible giant of the world." Sooner or later it will crush every good thing, and we will not even have seen it happen.

January 25: I am alienated when I don't know if life will be better tomorrow or not and I don't care.

"When people are serving," John Gardner wrote, "life is no longer meaningless." It is when we take more than we give that life satiates to the point of boredom.

January 26: I am out of touch with myself when I suppress my feelings to the point that I think I don't have any and so avoid having to cope with them.

January 27: I live a meaningful life when I measure what effect my behavior has on the universe. I live a significant one when I care enough to change my behaviors if they contribute more to human pain than to human progress. I live a holy one when I spend my life making connections between the way the system operates and the way people live.

January 28: The ultimate alienation is to be an American with no notion of what American foreign policy or economic systems do to people around the world. It is to live inside a national bubble in a global world and call it life. It is the ability to watch the starving and the dispossessed and the wounded on the television screens in our living rooms and never, ever set out to find out why they are in that situation.

January 29: "The great business of life is to be, to do, to do without, and to depart," John Morley wrote.

Meaning happens when we recognize each of these stages as they come upon us — and live them to the fullest.

January 30: When we fail to ask the great questions of life, we fail to understand the little ones.

January 31: A Jewish proverb reads: "What soap is for the body, tears are for the soul." If you have cried for nothing but yourself lately, there is something important in life that you are failing to see.

FEBRUARY

PSALM 112

Happy are those
who love God....
They are a light
in the darkness
for the upright;
they are generous,
merciful and just....
People such as these
will be honored.

*I*n a century that has spawned Adolf Hitler, Ferdinand Marcos, Nicolae Ceausescu, "The Terminator," and teenage gangs on one side, and Martin Luther King, Jr., Dan Berrigan, and Mahatma Gandhi on the other, we find ourselves confronted by what seem to be conflicting notions of leadership. Is it force or is it example that defines it? As a result, we have developed some very strange conceptions of what it means to be strong, effective, and publicly meaningful. Leadership has become an enigma. Are we to be faithful followers or independent individuals? Are leaders those who are trusted or feared?

The questions are cultural ones. In highly communitarian societies, it is extremely important to foster individualism so that people do not get swallowed up in the name of national development. In these situations leaders become martinets who use people for the sake of personal or social ideals that may not benefit the individuals whose lives are ground up in the project. The pharaohs built mighty pyramids but at the price of a million lives. The kings of Spain created a national treasury of American gold but at the price of entire native American populations.

In highly individualistic societies, like our own, it is just as important to foster a sense of group responsibility so that private interests do not usurp the common good. Corporate executives who take million-dollar salaries for themselves while their laid-off middle-class workers lose their homes to failed mortgages do not benefit society, though they affect it. Street gangs that terrorize neighborhoods to exert a power that is not theirs to use do not influence a society; they bully it. Family members who manipulate the environment for their own emotional needs, whatever the cost to those around them, control but they do not lead.

Leadership is the ability to pursue the greater good whether anyone else is going in that direction or not. It is, as the psalmist says, the ability "to be a light in the darkness for the upright." And it is often a lonely, lonely role.

Each of us knows in our heart what is the right road to follow. It is finding companions and pathbreakers on the way that is difficult.

February 1: Leadership is the ability to declare a thoughtful "no" in the face of a chorus of empty "yeses." It is the struggle between approval and conscience.

February 2: The function of a leader is not necessarily to have all the correct answers. Leaders are people who enable a group to ask the right questions early enough so that the group can answer them itself when the time comes.

February 3: "A leader," Napoleon said, "is a dealer in hope." It is not fair to speak of doomsday to a group unless we are prepared to help the group get beyond it. Anything else is simply negativism gone mad.

February 4: Leadership is not an interchangeable part that can be rotated at will. We do not "rotate" organists, computer programmers, or accountants. Leadership is a skill, a gift, a charism. Groups that want to succeed, to survive, need leadership. Groups that kill their leaders kill themselves.

February 5: The Chinese sage Lao-Tzu taught, "To lead the people, walk behind them." Leadership is the ability to enable a group to do what the group knows it must do.

February 6: Real leaders don't set out to organize a crowd. They simply set their faces in the right direction, regardless of how lonely the road, and one day discover that there is a crowd behind them.

February 7: It is not necessary to be in an official position in order to be a leader. It is only necessary to be brave, to be honest, and to be clear about where you are going and why. Thomas Merton was a spiritual leader who never left the monastery and never gave a retreat. The Beatles led a change in music styles, not by teaching music, but simply by doing something different with it themselves. Rosa Parks had gone to the back of the bus one too many times. The question is a simple one: What is it you believe in that you have failed to do anything about yet? Until you answer that question there is no proof that you are really a leader.

February 8: Don't confuse leadership with either authority or administration. Authority figures are often more devoted to preserving the present than constructing the future. Administrators keep their eye on the demands of the day rather than on the questions of the day. Leaders are thinkers who light the path for others by virtue of their clear vision, not of the future, but of the present and what must be done about it to maintain its dynamism.

February 9: The Korean proverb teaches: "Where there are no tigers, a wildcat is very self-important." It is very easy to confuse having a position with being a leader. Leaders make us ask the big questions and show us the answers to them in their own lives. Anything else is at best only a pale shadow of real leadership.

February 10: "Question authority, but raise your hand first," some wag wrote. There's wisdom to that, all right. People who set out to disrupt a system, to attack authority simply for the sake of calling attention to themselves, are not leaders. Leaders always respect authority. It is ideas they question.

February 11: The personal integrity of authority figures must be presumed at all times if dissent is to be faithful. The fact is that authority figures demonstrate their own integrity. It wasn't what the Chinese students in Tiananmen Square said about the Chinese government, for instance, that discredited it. It is what the world watched the government do to the students that soured its image.

February 12: Warren Bennis says, "Managers are people who do things right, and leaders are people who do the right things." Regardless of who likes it.

February 13: Leaders inspire people to lead themselves. Anything else is either errant parenting or dictatorship. The concept applies, it seems, to both church and state.

February 14: "There are only two powers in the world," Napoleon wrote, "the power of the sword and the power of the spirit. In the long run, the sword will always be conquered by the spirit." Force accomplishes nothing in the long run. Force may control a crowd but it cannot change its mind.

February 15: In the Soviet Union, freedom broke out; in the church, women are breaking out; in the world, the indigenous peoples are breaking out; in the cities, the poor are breaking out. The right voice at the right time and the old system will fall, not because it has been conquered by a malevolent force but because it has been destroyed by its own narrowness and the penetrating insights of leaders who are "generous, merciful, and just. . . . " The question is: Are you and I one of those leaders? Are we leading where we are or are we waiting for someone else to do it for us?

February 16: "To be a light in the darkness" is to ask the right question, say the right word, give the right answers in an environment that does not want to hear them.

February 17: "Do you have the book, *Man, Master of Women?*" the young man asked the librarian. "Yep," the clerk replied. "Second stack on your left — *Fiction.*"

February 18: The tragedy of life is to assume that what is must be. All it takes for change to happen is for someone to say aloud what every other person in the room knows in the silence of their hearts to be true but has not yet been able to articulate.

February 19: Leadership is never for its own sake. To lead for the sake of leading is ambition. Leadership sets out to empower others to achieve what they need but do not have.

February 20: Leaders are not cheerleaders, not crowd pleasers, not rebels for the sake of rebellion. Leaders are often solitary figures who do what needs to be done whether anyone else joins them on the spot or not. And sure enough, sooner or later, people do.

February 21: "It is true that force rules the world," Blaise Pascal wrote, "but opinion looses force." The most fundamental element of leadership is not social uproar, not confrontation, not rebellion. It is an idea whose validity is clear but whose consequences are unacceptable to the system that stands to lose from its acceptance.

February 22: "Why is it that wherever Jesus went there was a revolution" the apocryphal bishop is said to have lamented to his clergy, "but wherever I go, they pour tea?" The answer is obvious. Leadership has something do with bringing new light to the dark places in life, not in maintaining old ideas in the name of systemic nicety. As the psalmist says, "People such as these will be honored."

February 23: Ernest Bramah wrote, "The reputation of a thousand years may depend on the conduct of a single moment." It is what we do when it counts most that determines the quality of our leadership. To fail to act when the equality of a person, the hopes of a people, and the justice of the ages is in jeopardy is not only to lack leadership; it is to sin.

February 24: Leaders are not people who do great things for themselves. They are people who set out to do great things for others.

February 25: When scientists fail, we call it an "experiment" and applaud the process. When other people fail, we call it a mistake and warn them about making more of them. That's why as long as we're afraid to make a mistake, we'll never make the world a better place. That's also why the great social advances in life have all come out of what the rest of the world called foolishness, error, or heresy. The church put England under interdict for accepting the Magna Carta, governments jailed women for wanting to vote, society returned runaway slaves to lives of pain and punishment. Now tell me where leadership really lies?

February 26: The saddest sight in the world is people who confuse their authority with their ability to lead. It won't be long in such a situation before the real leaders in the group arise to chart a path beyond what has inevitably become static, confused, or self-serving. Then the horses start to pull in different directions.

February 27: A group in which leadership is suppressed by authority is a group that is doomed to an early death. Parishes dry up and shrivel, businesses decline, ideas go to straw, progress is replaced by stagnant systems. The most charismatic of groups will turn into mere shells of their former selves without acknowledged leadership.

February 28: Spiritual leadership incites a person to a wholeness of the soul that gives life quality — not to the keeping of laws without substance, ideas without sense, and rules without meaning.

MARCH

PSALM 85

*Mercy and
faithfulness meet;
justice and
peace embrace.
Faithfulness springs
from the earth,
and justice looks
down from heaven.*

This society is locked in mortal combat between mercy and justice. On which side must we err if err we must? Which side do we want for ourselves when we cut corners, bend the rules, break the codes, succumb to needs not being met in other places and ways? Which side is right?

We call the people who argue on behalf of mercy bleeding-heart liberals. We call the people who cry for more prisons, longer sentences, or capital punishment righteous types. What we never seem to consider, however, is that mercy and justice may be the same thing. What if they can't be separated? What must we do, then, when we judge others? As things stand now, we make enemies out of elements that must be inextricably linked if either is to function at all. We make opposites out of elements which, if separated, will each be weakened by the loss of its other dimension. We think that we must be one or the other instead of learning how to be both at the same time.

We forget that it can be merciful to restrain people from harming either themselves or others. We fail to remember that it can be the highest form of justice to practice mercy. Until, that is, one day we need them both ourselves. Until we examine our own lives and the lives of those we love and find them bathed in mercy where many would have said that justice was required. Then we understand God a little better. Then we understand both mercy and justice in a different way.

March 1: The strangest of all human phenomena, perhaps, is that we all take God's mercy for granted for ourselves but find it so hard to be merciful to others. If there were any proof needed that God is completely "Other," this is surely it.

March 2: G. K. Chesterton wrote, "Children are innocent and love justice, while most adults are wicked and prefer mercy." Right. By the time we grow up we realize how awful a thing justice really is when it is devoid of mercy.

March 3: What is justice but the ability to mete out what is deserved? That's why justice and mercy are one. We are made of dust, not gold, remember? And dust is worthy of little but mercy. Now that is great luck.

March 4: Justice gives the unworthy what would be their due if they were worthy. Mercy gives the unworthy exactly what they most need. Who said God didn't make us to have it both ways?

March 5: Justice is often confused with righteousness. Justice requires us to take every slightest mitigating factor of an event into account. Justice sees the motive, the might, and the need. Righteousness sees only the law.

March 6: The poet José Martí wrote, "When others are weeping blood, what right have I to weep tears?" Real justice requires that we commiserate with those who suffer so that we can find the reason within us to put an end to the oppression.

March 7: Mercy is what makes a person human; justice is what makes a person think.

March 8: When people feel deprived from without they cry for justice; when they feel powerless within they cry for mercy.

March 9: People consider mercy a gift but justice a birthright. Consequently, people never expect mercy but they will eventually, always, demand justice.

March 10: "Injustice never rules forever," the Roman philosopher Seneca wrote. Injustice is at the base of every revolution in history. The lesson is clear: a country that wants a safe and stable future will treat its poorest members very well.

March 11: Justice we take for granted. Mercy obliges us forever. That's why the justice of God is not to be feared: God's judgment will take everything about us into account — and God's mercy gives us always more than we expected. So we keep trying.

March 12: "Who is closer to God," the seeker asked, "the saint or the sinner?" "Why, the sinner, of course," the elder said. "But how can that be?" the seeker asked. "Because," the elder said, "every time we sin we break the cord that binds us to God. But every time God forgives us, the cord is knotted again. And so, thanks to the mercy of God, the cord gets shorter and the sinner closer to God." It's true, isn't it? We learn from sin the goodness of God — and then our shame is exceeded only by our love.

March 13: Justice and judgment are not synonyms. Justice requires restitution for wrong. Judgment marks and labels and refuses either to forgive or to forget.

March 14: It is so easy to speak fondly of being merciful to the poor and disenfranchised in the society. What is difficult is to do justice for them because it would require so many changes in our own lives.

March 15: To receive mercy from someone else is to learn humility. To extend mercy to others is to learn something about the nature of God. It is very hard to say which learning is more important.

March 16: Sir William Blackstone, legendary English barrister, wrote, "It is better that ten guilty persons escape than that one innocent suffer." But if we believed that, we would not be one of the countries in the world that practices capital punishment in the name of justice. Some hallmark for a nation that calls itself Christian.

March 17: "What are you in prison for?" Mother Jones, the old labor organizer, is said to have asked the poor young unemployed man in the cell. "For stealing $50," the young man answered. "Too bad you didn't steal a railroad," she replied. "You could be in the Senate by now." It makes you think, doesn't it? How did blue-collar crime get to be the scourge of the nation and white-collar crime just one of the vagaries of business? It is a question worth pursuing. The answer could tell us more than we may want to know about our society, about ourselves, and about our standards of both justice and mercy.

March 18: "Justice ... limps along, but it gets there all the same," the novelist Gabriel García Márquez wrote. Things have a way of catching up with us. Too much alcohol ends in liver disease. Too much anger ends in heart trouble. Too little mercy ends in isolation. Every minute of every day we make for ourselves either justice or mercy.

March 19: "Humankind's true moral test," Milan Kundera wrote, "its fundamental test (which lies deeply buried from view), consists of its attitude towards those who are at its mercy: animals. And in this respect humankind has suffered a fundamental debacle, a debacle so fundamental that all others stem from it." Think about it: what humans do to animals, to those most in need of human mercy, is a measure of the way we will treat others. If one form of life is disposable, available for torture and neglect, devoid of value in our eyes, then life itself, all life, is in danger from us. Maybe that's why God brought each animal to Adam. Not to give him the right to kill them but to make him see that he was in relationship with them as well. If so, we have missed the message to the peril of the globe.

March 20: Mercy adds love to punishment. Justice adds value to life.

March 21: There is a distinct difference between justice and vengeance. Vengeance is a wrong greater than the wrong that provoked it because vengeance emerges out of a kind of justice that sets out to repair evil by evil.

March 22: To do justice requires that we give people what they need, not simply what they earn. For a company that can afford more, to justify paying low wages on the grounds that people knew the pay scale when they took the job is to force people into the new industrial slavery. And it will eventually have the same effect as slavery.

March 23: "When George Washington admitted to his father that he chopped down the cherry tree, he didn't get whipped because he told the truth," the boy shouted from across his father's knee. "Well, I told you that I pushed the outhouse into the creek, Pa, so why are you whipping me?" "Because, son," his father shouted back, hand poised above him, "when George Washington chopped down the cherry tree, his father wasn't sitting in it at the time!" Point: Don't presume on mercy when justice is in order. At least not from anyone but God.

March 24: The only way to assure justice is to administer it always with mercy.

March 25: Righteous anger is a holy thing. It fuels us for the journey to justice. Nevertheless, when anger consumes us, justice disappears.

March 26: Mercy and justice are not the virtues of children. They must be learned by long years of failure. Then, the compassion that comes out of self-knowledge takes over and we do justice tenderly, aware always of our own weaknesses.

March 27: The bruised reed shall not be bent, Benedict admonishes the abbot in his sixth-century Rule. What good does it do to exact the kind of justice that breaks the spirit and sours the heart?

March 28: There is an element of the Christian tradition which argues that capital punishment is wrong because by cutting off life prematurely we make it impossible for a person to grow, to repent, and to develop full stature. It's an important consideration. By punishing a person to make things better we may actually be stopping that person from becoming better and making things worse ourselves. These are the kinds of questions that have to be asked if we are going to take the concepts of mercy and justice seriously. Before it's over, what we think about this question may mark the measure of the mercy and justice that we ourselves deserve.

March 29: "Vengeance is mine. I will repay," says God. But we so much want to do it ourselves, don't we? Is that because we don't trust God or because, though we prefer mercy for ourselves, we want justice for others. And come to think about it, you'd hate to trust God in a situation like that.

March 30: "God does not punish sin . . . ," the mystic Julian of Norwich teaches. "Sin punishes sin." It makes sense. If greed is our sin, we shall be forever intent on having more. If anger is our sin, we will be consumed by emotional imbalance. If lust is our sin, we will be forever unsatiated. If sloth is our sin, we will never know achievement or success. No one can ever punish us as much as the internal turmoil that we create by our own lack of control.

March 31: Someone will irritate you today. Be kind in return. Then ask yourself what happened inside you as a result. Surprise.

APRIL

Psalm 43

Send your light
and your truth;
let these be my guide.
Lead me to
your holy mountain,
to the place
where you dwell.

*T*he dark spots in life — those times when the present seems unbearable and the future seems impossible — appear often to be empty, useless moments. It's only later, when we look back, that we can see how really rich those periods were for us. Darkness, in fact, is the beginning of light. It is the one place where we are obliged to see what we have never been willing or able to understand before. Darkness is spiritual ambiguity, holy contradiction, disarming mystery. The one major function of darkness in this world, whatever kind of darkness it may be, is always, in the final analysis, enlightenment. What we learn when we cannot see our way through a hard place in life are insights that we have failed to discern in better situations. When life is good we don't look as closely perhaps. When life is easy, we don't listen at all. When life is difficult, we have the sense to wonder why. We hear a great deal about loss in life, for instance, but we never really come to know intangible presence until someone we really love dies. We read one article after another on simplicity of life but we never really come to realize how little it takes to be happy until we lose something of great significance. Enlightenment is the moment in life when we have little left outside ourselves and sud-

denly discover something inside ourselves that compensates for all of it.

Philosophers and theologians debate eternally what every human being, one way or another, comes to know without doubt: life is a process of watching the material dimensions of the human condition slip away while the spirit grows stronger, greater, richer all the way to eternity. All the while our bodies wane, the spirit is waxing. It is the paradox of life. That's why no one is ever ready to die. The older we get the more we are just beginning to understand life and to really live it well. That process is called enlightenment.

April 1: The strange thing about life is that when we are most immersed in the material things of life we are often least aware of the spiritual. When we are clamoring for more of everything we can see, we are seeing least.

April 2: Enlightenment comes when there seems to be no help whatsoever for our present predicament. Then we come to realize that predicaments are not predicaments at all. They are simply turns in the road toward home, toward becoming the person we were always meant to be but never were challenged enough to become.

April 3: When the obstacles of life feel implacable, when we are frustrated beyond all measure trying to change the circumstances around us but can't, then it is time to ask what it is in this particular situation that we are refusing to learn.

April 4: Never think that darkness is the end of anything. It is simply the call to a new beginning.

April 5: There are moments in life when everything we've ever worked for, waited for, planned for, saved for, crumbles and dies and fails. The job goes, the money runs out, a child dies, the family breaks down, the business collapses — the dreams of a lifetime break into pieces. Darkness is the feeling. Despair is the temptation. Freedom is the hope. If I can just cling to life trustingly, that is enlightenment. After that, there is nothing whatsoever I can ever lose again that can destroy me.

April 6: It is precisely when the distractions of life fall away that the consciousness of soul takes over and God, here, now, in the middle of me, becomes real, becomes true. Then, God, that which cannot be grasped, becomes the only thing really graspable. If God is allowed to fill the gap, the soul soars free and life is full again.

April 7: It isn't that the pain of loss goes away; it is simply that we put down the pain. The core of the soul lets go of the things in life that go through our fingers like sand and clings instead to the formless things of life that have neither a beginning nor an end: beauty, the seasons of life, the Word that enriches, the cultivation of the inner rather than the outer life.

April 8: Jonathan Swift wrote, "May you live all the days of your life." How rarely that is done. Most of us live half of today waiting for some nebulous tomorrow instead of enjoying what is in front of us right now.

April 9: To have something as if we did not have it at all: now that is enlightenment.

April 10: The mystic Mechtild of Magdeburg defines enlightenment best, I think. She says that the purpose of life is "to see God in all things and all things in God." When that happens there is no darkness left.

April 11: Don't be afraid of darkness. It is simply an invitation to new light.

April 12: When we cannot see our way out of darkness, it is because there is more light there than we have yet come to realize. Every darkness brings its own message, after which we are never again the people we were before the darkness came.

April 13: Fortunately we do not get everything we ever wanted in life. If we did, we would never wonder why. The answer to why is always the meaning of life for us.

April 14: The Hindu holy scriptures read: "The way is not in the sky; the way is in the heart." We are so prone to look for answers outside ourselves. Sometimes it's because we don't like the answers we find within us; sometimes it's because we don't understand them. In either case, the answers outside ourselves are simply information. The answers within us are the voice of God calling us to truths we know to be essential to our peace of mind but do not want to face. The day we do, that will be enlightenment.

April 15: The psychologist Carl Jung tried to teach the world that there is a light side and a dark side, a dark side and a light side to everything. No matter where you are in life now, in darkness or in light, enlightenment involves considering what its opposite would demand of us. Then we'll know what life requires of us to complete the present process.

April 16: Dogen writes, "Do not think you will necessarily be aware of your own enlightenment." Sometimes the purpose of our enlightenment is to be a light to others which we ourselves do not consciously comprehend. If we live well, in other words, we become the light that others need. So is our own enlightenment wasted on us? No, not if we remember to drain every day of its meaning.

April 17: What is enlightenment? It is exactly what the psalmist says it is: it is an awareness of light and truth in us, so strong, so clear, that it leads us beyond anything that would disturb our peace.

April 18: We know that enlightenment has occurred when what bothered us in the past now has no power whatsoever over us.

April 19: Etty Hillesum, a Jewish concentration camp victim, wrote, "To live fully, outwardly and inwardly, not to ignore external reality for the sake of the inner life, or the reverse — that's quite a task." It is also the only real task in life.

April 20: The raw material of enlightenment is only ourselves — not what we have, not what we do — only what we are, down deep and real, when everything else has gone to straw.

April 21: Enlightenment comes to those who open themselves to the meaning of every event, the potential of every action, the beauty of every simple moment in life. It is rare wisdom, this, in a people who go through life at the speed of sound.

April 22: How shall we recognize enlightenment? Enlightenment is the moment at which the need for things falls away. Enlightenment is the moment at which we put the great hurts of life behind us and embrace the new with all our energy, with all our heart. Enlightenment is the moment at which we discover that the fullness of life is in the first great music we are able to hum, the first flower bud we look for and find, the first person we love without expecting to be loved in return.

April 23: Never fear periods of darkness in life. They are the atrium to new phases of life, the threshold to new experience, the invitation to move on from where you are to where there is more for you to learn.

April 24: The problem with the Western world is that we think in ladders. The assumption is that if we are not going "up" we are going nowhere at all or, worse, into oblivion. The real truth is that "down" is often "up" and "nowhere" is sometimes the best place of all.

April 25: The Indian philosopher Sadhu Vaswani suggests the following as a motto for all educational institutions: "Oh Wanderer, thy homeland seeketh Thee." The really enlightened know the truth of that.

The rest of us are still dense enough to think we're seeking it.

April 26:   Enlightenment is not the monopoly of monasteries. On the contrary. Those are enlightened who find God where they are — and recognize the Presence in others as well.

April 27:   Thank God for whatever darkness you have gone through. Without it, you would never know the difference between darkness and light.

April 28:   Darkness is not imposed on us; it is in us. Whatever is darkness for each of us right now comes from the fact that we refuse to let go of what we want in order to accept the gift at hand. Enlightenment is freedom.

April 29:   Enlightenment does not always imply the achievement of a new situation in life. More likely, it consists simply of seeing the old circumstances in a new way. "Discovery," Albert Szent-Gyorg wrote, "consists of seeing what everybody has seen and thinking what nobody has thought."

April 30:   "Master, I come to you seeking enlightenment," the priest said to the Holy One. "Well, then," the master said, "for the first exercise of your retreat, go into the courtyard, tilt back your head, stretch out your arms and wait until I come for you." Just as the priest arranged himself in the garden, the rain came. And it rained. And it rained. And it rained. Finally, the old master came back. "Well, priest," he said. "Have you been enlightened today?" "Are you serious?" the priest said in disgust. "I've been standing here with my head up in the rain for an hour. I'm soaking wet, and I feel like a fool!" And the master said, "Well, priest, for the first day of a retreat that sounds like great enlightenment to me."

MAY

PSALM 27

Caught up
in your beauty,
I speak of
my heart's desire;
to find
the fullness of life,
dwelling in your
presence forever.

A sixth-century document, The Rule of Benedict, designed to point the way to fullness of life, is quite clear: we all must be known by somebody wise enough, caring enough, balanced enough to help us know ourselves. Benedict calls it the Fourth Degree of Humility. The implication is that if we fail to work through the thoughts, the ideas, the pains that consume us we can't grow beyond them. We need to learn to trust, to share, to admit our weaknesses, to take off our masks, to be in the world with honesty and authenticity. That doesn't mean that we tell everyone everything. It means that we must tell someone everything. That's why choosing friends is so important. That's why allowing someone into our lives is key to our own development. Intimacy is not a condition, it is a necessity of human growth.

May 1: If there is one problem with intimacy, it's got to be that we ask more of relationships — either married or single — than they can ever give. The function of a relationship is to enhance life, not to complete it. When we ask more of the people who love us than we provide for ourselves, we set ourselves up for emotional disaster.

May 2: To tell others too much too soon is to expect them to carry our lives for us before they themselves care as much about our lives as they do their own.

May 3: Physical intimacy has little or nothing to do with the kind of intimacy that takes care of the heart. Physical intimacy is an expression of chemistry; emotional intimacy is an expression of total trust, total concern. The first kind of intimacy is spontaneous. The other kind, the important kind, is rare and long in coming.

May 4: "I felt it shelter to speak to you," Emily Dickinson wrote. Perhaps there is no better way to describe the real effects of intimacy. Those who are our intimates are those with whom we are safe and respected, regardless of how small we may seem to ourselves at the time. The question is whether or not any of us have ever fully lived until we have known such comfort.

May 5: Intimacy does not depend on geography. It depends on honesty, support, and emotional presence. If we depend on others simply to provide a distraction for us from the routine of life, that is companionship, not friendship.

May 6: We can be intimate only with those whom we allow to be themselves. Intimacy is not the right to control another; it is simply the expectation that we can trust the other in our behalf. We can tell the other half of our soul to those with whom we can be intimate, knowing that it will never under any circumstances be used against us and that they can do the same with us.

May 7: If there is no one in life with whom we are completely honest — completely — then there is no one in life we really love.

May 8: When intimacy ends, and it can, the trust that glued it together does not dissolve; it simply ceases to be meaningful in the present. If you love well to begin with, that love is safe even when it comes to the point where it takes a new shape. Anything else is not just uncaring; it is despicable because it betrays a trust once true.

May 9: Relationships fade when one person has to bear too much of the life of the other person.

May 10: When we take responsibility for creating our own happiness rather than tying it to the presence of another person, we are more fit than ever to be a part of someone else's life. Then we have more to bring to that person than our own needs.

May 11: Kahlil Gibran wrote: "Let there be space in your togetherness." Try distance and you will discover yourself — your own ideas, your own abilities, your own interests, your own internal resources.

May 12: It's one thing to love companionship. It's another to be unable to function without it.

May 13: If we're not careful, life can have a way of getting smaller and smaller as the years go by. We go to the same places with the same people and talk about the same things over and over again. At that point, it's time to go somewhere else, join something new, try something else, meet someone new before our lives develop a kind of emotional sclerosis that stops our hearts and shrinks our minds.

May 14: Sometimes the best thing that can happen to a relationship is a good fight. It's a test of whether we're still alive enough to function on our own. If so, we can both learn from the relationship; if not, this relationship has become too dull to continue and is no more than a cardboard copy of the real thing.

May 15: I used to know a bishop who would say in the middle of a long evening of talk, "It's time to go home. There is nothing to learn here; everyone agrees." It's an attitude in search of an institution these days.

May 16: Beware the marriage that's all him or all her. It may look idyllic, but it has long ago ceased to be love.

May 17: The person who loves me intimately loves me for myself. The person who claims to love me but keeps insisting that I be something other than I am, do something other than I can without bartering my own responsibilities, or think something other than I truly believe is not looking for a friend. That person is looking for a pet.

May 18: "I am His Majesty's dog at Kew; pray tell me, Sir, whose dog are you?" the English poet Alexander Pope wrote. It's amazing the number of persons, institutions, clubs, and social castes that will try to tame us for themselves as we go through life. The trick to living is to keep our minds free, even of our friends. Anything else is brain death, not intimacy.

May 19: Our most intimate friends are the ones who can help us work toward our best selves, not confirm us in our weakest selves. The way to tell one from another is to disagree. Try it someday. If you lose a friend, you will have gained a life.

May 20: Han Suyin, a Eurasian author, wrote: "Love from one being to another can only be that two solitudes come nearer, recognize and protect and comfort each other." That kind of love is a rare, rare situation depending on two equally adult and self-confident people.

May 21: Beware what you expect in a friend. You may be saddling yourself with a burden you will not be able to put down in the future. It is one thing to meet people who are inclined to be dependent and set out to teach them to trust themselves. It is another thing to make people dependent on us to enhance our own sense of control. That will eventually diminish both their life and ours.

May 22: Intimacy is that point in a relationship when another person knows me at least as well as I know myself — and accepts what I am without judgment. It does not imply that the other person accepts in me less than everything of which I'm capable.

May 23: If you want a real friendship, don't give directions to those you love. You are not their mother; you are their friend. Listen to them, help them to explore themselves, enable them to weigh the effects of the things they're doing. But don't put them in a position to need your approval for anything. That is not intimacy; that is destructive of the person of another and eventually it will sour the relationship.

May 24: Those who really love me are there when I need them, free when I don't, undemanding at all times.

May 25: An interesting exercise in life is to look at all the characteristics of intimacy that are presented here, then think of all the things I myself hope for in another and ask myself if I am giving to anyone else what I want for myself.

May 26: The painter Claude Monet wrote: "I perhaps owe having become a painter to flowers." There's a lesson in that statement, I think. Do we love anything else enough to say that it has truly changed, shaped, formed our own life? If not, have we ever loved at all?

May 27: We are not, the psalmist is clear, a world unto ourselves. "To find the fullness of life," we must go out of ourselves to find the Divine Presence in the other. The awareness of beauty beyond ourselves calls us to become more than we can possibly be alone.

May 28: To use people for our own gratification, purpose, advancement and call that intimacy is obscene. We can only really be intimate with those whom we let into our lives to make our lives honest.

May 29: "Am I united with my friend in heart / What matters if our place be wide apart?" the Persian poet Anwar-I-Suheili wrote. An intimate friend is more than a companion. Anybody can be that. An intimate friend is the one who has more to do with my heart than my schedule.

May 30: Beware people who won't give you space for more friends, other activities, new ideas, and unrelated experiences. They are a lot more interested in themselves than they are in you.

May 31: The essayist Montaigne wrote, "If you press me to say why I loved him, I can say no more than it was because he was he, and I was I." It is being able to be myself that is the test of intimacy. Only God has the right to form us in ways we would not go.

JUNE

PSALM 103

*As parents are tender
with their children,
so God is gentle
with those who believe.*

*T*he concept of "family" is a very different, a very difficult, concept for us in this culture today. We have been raised, many of us, in a society of uniracial, one-denominational families where fathers were the "breadwinners" and mothers were "housewives," where colors did not mix and women as a class were economically dependent. Divorce was socially unacceptable. Women were legal minors. Childbearing was a basically uncontrollable process. It was our ideal of the perfect home.

We mourn the loss of those ideal structures and, for many reasons, rightly so. The number of single-parent homes is on the increase. The number of merged families leaves children with two part-time families rather than one full-time family. Childhood poverty is multiplying at an alarming rate in the richest country in the world. Marriage, in too many cases, has become a very tentative venture. We are inclined, as a result, to see earlier forms of family life as perfect, despite the fact that those periods, too, produced great suffering, even great sin. People lived in loveless marriages all their lives. Children were unwanted, ignored, abused, and deprived. Women and children were abandoned with impunity, made poor or forced to cope with countless infidelities. Whether the *ideal was ever truly real becomes a question of great social import.*

At the same time, we have been so concerned about the emergence of various forms of modern families — biracial, single-parent, merged, mixed, blended, and single-sex — that we have too often lost sight of the underlying essence of human relationships. When we pray, "God of Love," we forget that God's love takes no form, has no boundaries, knows no barriers, requires no systemic litmus test of propriety. We forget that God's love is unconditional and so requires the same of us. We have forgotten that only love can make a family.

But the psalmist knows better. The psalmist talks only and always of the God who is tender, the God who brooks no obstacles to covenant, the God who bars no color, no status, no social caste, no sex from the fullness of life because this God puts love above law. The psalmist makes us examine every relationship for the quality that maintains it, not the legalities that define it or the structures that shape it.

If we are to become God's family — the human family — we must surely do the same, praying only that every family, whatever its form, will have the resources it needs to live in dignity and in love and the spirituality it needs to live always with integrity, tenderness, and laughter.

June 1: Families are more than legal units. A family is a web of those whose lives entwined can never be separated no matter the distance, no matter how hard they try.

June 2: "Happiness," George Burns says, "is having a large, loving, caring, close-knit family—in another city." That way you can cross the country without having to worry about motel bills. I mean, what else are families for!

June 3: The function of family is to make us feel secure enough in one world to be able to venture confidently into another. Too often it is the family itself that breaks down the sense of self, that fails to nourish the gifts of each, that brings sarcasm, criticism, and control into the home. When a family produces people who hurt, people who are angry, people filled with self-hate, those people years later do the same to others in order to ease the pain of their own sense of inadequacy. If we want a peaceful world, it will have to start in the home.

June 4: "Home," Robert Frost wrote, "is the place where, when you go there, they have to take you in." The point is clear: for a house to be a home to you, you must be always, eternally welcome anywhere you are.

June 5: Daniel Berrigan says, "Children are our most endangered species." Yes, but children are the only proof we have that tomorrow can be holy, can be beautiful. If children are being abused in this culture, it is because this culture is abusive. Until we begin to make the connections between guns, militarism, more money for prisons and less money for schools, it will only get worse. It's time to elect politicians who make society better instead of people who simply make prison terms longer. To talk "family values" while ignoring public values is to fool ourselves.

June 6: "Making the decision to have a child," Elizabeth Stone wrote, "is momentous. It is to decide forever to have your heart go walking around outside your body." And she was correct — but incomplete in the concept. All children, whether ours or not, are the carriers of the life we leave behind for them. In every child alive resides the consequences of the policies, the consciences of us all.

June 7: Before the industrial revolution and the development of the nuclear family — the custom of restricting the definition of family to one set of adults and their children — raising children was a community responsibility. All children were raised in extended families, in families made up of grandparents, uncles, aunts, and cousins. Raising children, in other words, was a community affair, not the responsibility of a single pair of parents. Before we too quickly criticize parents for what they do not do for their children, maybe we each need to ask ourselves what we are doing to meet our own responsibility to their children.

June 8: To be without a family is to be without the assurance that there is, somewhere in the world, someone who is required to love us. Then we are forced to learn to trust the rest of the human race.

June 9: "Children need models rather than critics," Joseph Joubert wrote. The implication is a simple one: What do you want for children? Are you doing it yourself?

June 10: The Sufi say, "Never try to teach a pig to sing. It will frustrate you — and it will irritate the pig." Tell me again: what good does nagging do?

June 11: There is a child in all of us who needs to be protected, cared for, nurtured, valued. Who takes care of the child in you — and whose soul child are you loving to life? Whoever it is, the soul child is really your family — regardless of whom you are legally related to.

June 12: Adoption is the way we go out of ourselves in the gratuitous love of God. There is no love more strong, more pure, more holy than the love of the parent who does not need to love us — but does.

June 13: We love children, we say, and we sacralize motherhood, but 80 percent of the refugees of the world today are women and children. What are you saying about that?

June 14: There are families everywhere struggling with their family's secret — poverty, division, alcoholism, abuse — and smiling, smiling, smiling on the outside. Open your arms today. Take everyone in. Half the people you see are bearing a secret too big for them to bear alone.

June 15: When we cheer the welfare "reform" that denies the children of non-working parents food stamps, whatever we say about children becomes bad poetry, a living lie, a blight on the future of our own families who will live with the social consequences of an underdeveloped society. Point: think carefully before you applaud.

June 16: The English poet Alexander Pope wrote: "'Tis education forms the common mind: / just as the twig is bent, the tree's inclined." If we want strong families in the United States, it may be time to give less attention to reforming the welfare system and put more attention on reforming our schools.

June 17: Sexism destroys the family because it assumes that the function of one person in the family is to make life convenient, possible, and free for everyone else in the family, with no attention to themselves. That's not a "family"; that's a group with a servant. Just like in the old days.

June 18: Where there is love and dignity, a family exists — whether that loving group meets past definitions of family or not.

June 19: A family is not made by a document. A family is made by custom, time, tradition, ideals — and tenderness.

June 20: Wherever there is love, there is family — the coming together of God's children under God's impulse.

June 21: Don't ever be afraid to be tender. Tenderness is a bond thicker than blood, surer than eternity, more promising than power. Tenderness says that we are looking for another — and have ourselves been found.

June 22: We grow beyond family but never out of it. The result is that a good family lets us be free but never so free that any distance — no matter how great — really separates us.

June 23: In every family there are people on the edge of it — geographically distant, ashamed, angry, or restrained by something outside their control that keeps them away. Who is it in your family? Think of what a call, a card, a small gift in a tiny envelope from you could do to bridge those distances. Ah, go ahead, risk it. You may just find yourself with a real family if you do.

June 24: It's amazing the things that we allow to wrench families apart: religion, marriage, homophobia, jealousy, money. That's like fighting over crumbs at a banquet table.

June 25: Somebody somewhere down the street, in the local nursing home, at the prison, in a tiny walk-up apartment has not a single living soul to visit them, send mail, or ring the phone. If you really believe in "family" you could adopt such a person. Having a family is not nearly as important in this day and age as being family to those who have none.

June 26: It is so easy to romanticize the pre-'60s family as ideal. From that model we know exactly how families should be structured, what they should do, how they should raise their children. We are certain that there should be two adults, of the same color, different genders, one religion, and separate roles. The only thing funny about the hypothesis is that that's exactly the generation who bred this one. Makes you wonder, doesn't it?

June 27: Families don't look like the old Dick and Jane books anymore. Some people think that's a sign that the world is falling apart. On the other hand, wouldn't it surprise us all if that turns out to be the very thing that brings us all together.

June 28: Motherhood is wonderful and fathering is grand but, social scientists tells us, parenting is better. Children who are raised — dressed, bathed, fed, played with, read to, and talked with — by both parents, the research indicates, are more flexible in life, more successful at work, more filled with self-esteem, more creative than either boys or girls who come from homes organized along sexual stereotypes. What's that saying? It may be saying that to realize the potential in ourselves we need to see possibility affirmed by both parents.

June 29: The less we let the world outside ourselves into our private, antiseptic little lives, the more narrow, less real we ourselves become. If you want to talk about the "human family," you will have to do something to create it. Develop a friendship with someone from another race, another religion, another sexual orientation, another economic level, another country. Until we do, we can never grow beyond ourselves.

June 30: To talk about the tenderness of God is to assume that there, in God's heart, everyone is welcome, everyone is loved, everyone is struggling to be whole, everyone is, at heart, good. That's family.

JULY

Psalm 47

*God is the Creator
of all the earth,
caring for all nations.*

*T*here are two concepts in U.S. history that deserve to be revisited if the Fourth of July is to have any meaning at all for the next century. The first is "patriotism." The second is "jingoism." They are not synonyms, as much as we are sometimes inclined to make them so. Patriotism is love of country — literally, the "father" land. Jingoism is chauvinism, a love of country that lacks a critical eye. Or better yet, perhaps, a love of country that lacks a loving eye. When we "love" something to such a degree that we lose the capacity to compare it to its own best potential, we don't really "love" it at all. We idolize it.

Jingoism is destructive idolatry, the kind of national fetish which can, if taken to its limit, end in the holocaust of Jews, the genocide of Bosnians, the decimation of Palestinians, and the massacre of Native Americans. But the psalmist is clear. God "cares for all nations." What we do in the name of "Americanism" to people will be weighed in the light of what is good for all creation, what is good not only for ourselves but also for those whose lives as a nation we touch.

Patriotism, on the other hand, is a commitment to the ideals for which, as a people, we say we strive. Real patriotism welcomes, encourages, commits itself to *the great national debates that question war, resist taxes, and determine penal systems.*

Patriotism asks hard questions: Are we really putting enough money into education in this country? Is eight weeks of training enough to provide people on welfare with the skills they need to find and maintain employment after we have cut off food stamps to their children? What exactly does an ethic of life require at all levels, at all times? Should we still be putting over half the national budget into the military establishment in peacetime? Those questions engage the patriot with honesty and courage. Those questions and others just as difficult, just as scalding, will determine the real direction of this country in the new millennium.

July 1: "I don't measure America by its achievement, but by its potential," Shirley Chisholm said. That's an inspiring ideal, of course, but an even better one may be to measure the entire globe, not by its achievement but by its potential. Until Indian children, Rwandan children, inner-city children are as safe, as well fed, with as much opportunity as children in our suburbs, human achievement lags and lacks and dies. Real patriotism understands that the health of this country depends on the well-being of the rest of the world, that what happens to one of us, happens to all of us as well.

July 2: Real patriotism will not be reached on this planet until, for each of us, our country is the world. Until then, we are all merely tribes fighting for territory that doesn't belong to us in the first place.

July 3: Unless all of us, both individually and as a nation, are committed to something that is good for the whole world as well as for ourselves, all the political talk about peace will be forever bogus. Then all we will ever have is armed truce.

July 4: Why is it that on the Fourth of July we celebrate nothing but our military victories? The Constitution of the United States is not about war: it is about the triumph of democracy, that state of public affairs where everyone has the right to disagree in peace.

July 5: The novelist Charlotte Brontë wrote, "I'm a universal patriot, if you could understand me rightly: my country is the world." Who of us can possibly say the same? And why not? Now that's the real question: Why not?

July 6: It is only when we travel outside our country that we can really come to know what it means to be from the United States. It is exhilarating — and humiliating. Real love of country demands that we find the beauty in other cultures and strive to grow from what we learn from others. As Albert Camus says, "I love my country too much to be a nationalist."

July 7: To be a citizen of the United States is to be a person whose culture has been formed from all the major nations of the earth. Our task is not to foster divisions on the basis of our varied backgrounds but to bring together the best from each with respect and dignity.

July 8: The virtue of patriotism demands that we put our founding ideals above our present opportunities. Otherwise, like all the decayed regimes before us, we may well put our national politics before our national character. "Patriotism," George Jean Nathan wrote, "is often an arbitrary veneration of real estate above principles."

July 9: Thomas Jefferson said it all for us. He wrote: "I tremble for my country when I reflect that God is just." And tremble we must in the face of a history full of slavery, of Indian reservations and broken treaties, of religious prejudice and the jailing of suffragettes, the women — our grandmothers — who were called "radical feminists" because they wanted women to have the right to vote. Power always tends to institutionalize itself. It is patriotism's greatest enemy.

July 10: Patriotism is a Christian question. It requires us to determine how much of ourselves we can commit to the glory of the state when other values — human rights, personal freedom, religious conscience, human dignity, or individual liberty — must be sacrificed in whatever measures to achieve it. "To make us love our country," Edmund Burke wrote, "our country ought to be lovely."

July 11: Patriotism is no justification for arrogance. The Super Race theory is simply patriotism gone mad. But the seed of the theory does not rest with governments. It grows like a hothouse plant in the hearts of individuals who concede the democratic process to political parties, the vote to their neighbors, the military budget to the Pentagon, and the declaration of war to presidents. Real patriots keep asking questions that refuse easy answers.

July 12: "My country, right or wrong, my country," sings of everything that democracy is not. That's precisely the formula that would have made the Declaration of Independence impossible. Instead, the United States of America was envisioned by thinkers, bequeathed to thinkers, and depends on thinkers for its continued development. When we cede our obligation to think things through ourselves in this country, the democratic experiment is over. All the parades in the world will not save it.

July 13: Clarence Darrow, the "Scopes Trial Lawyer," wrote: "True patriotism hates injustice in its own land more than anywhere else." What we do not preserve in this country we can never preach to anyone else.

July 14: Cory Aquino, liberating president of the Philippines, said something to me in her presidential office that seared my soul: "You Americans have two civil rights policies," she said. "One you apply inside your country; the other you apply to everyone else." I've never been able to forget it. What do you think that's saying? What does it have to do with patriotism?

July 15: The philosopher José Ortega y Gasset wrote: "What makes a nation great is not primarily its great men and women, but the stature of its innumerable mediocre ones." That's us. We're the ones who are responsible for the character of this country. Every time I hear someone say, "Well, you have to assume that the politicians know best what to do," I realize that one more person has surrendered citizenship for childish obedience.

July 16: The spirituality of patriotism demands that we "render unto Caesar the things that are Caesar's" — and not one thing more.

July 17: "Give me your tired, your poor, / Your huddled masses yearning to breathe free, / The wretched refuse of your teeming shore, / Send these, the homeless, tempest-tossed, to me: / I lift my lamp beside the golden door." Think of your great-grandparents while we refurbish the Statue of Liberty at one end of the country and build a better fence at the other end against the people we allow to do the work that we no longer want to do.

July 18: What would happen in U.S. high schools if we started to teach a history course built around our mistakes instead of concentrating on our military victories?

July 19: The United States participates in UN military engagements but does not pay its UN dues. What is that saying about being a citizen of the world, a U.S. patriot, a Christian? Somebody better figure it all out or we may be running the risk of being none of those. Which one comes first in your mind?

July 20: We used to fly a world flag over a U.S. flag at the monastery. They called it "communist" and a state congressperson called to tell us that there was a law against flying any flag above the U.S. flag. So we flew the world flag on Monday, Wednesday, and Friday and the U.S. flag on Tuesday, Thursday, and Saturday and no flag at all on Sunday, the Lord's Day. It was a respectful political compromise but it may not have been essentially Christian. Surely any country that considers itself above the planet puts the country in trouble and the planet in woe. What kind of a law is that? And what does it foster in a world that is getting smaller every day? And what does it require of the Christian in all of us?

July 21: Prejudice is anti-patriotic in a nation that is built on differences — yours, mine, and ours.

July 22: The United States does not have a long cultural past; it has a long pluralistic future. Or it can have, provided that "patriotism" remains a principle of universal commitment rather than a narrow political tool. We cannot simply preserve what is; we must honor what was and enable what can be for everyone, everywhere.

July 23: If we celebrate the military and forget the democratic and separate what it means to be a Christian from what it means to be a citizen, we are a country susceptible to demagogues to provide our ideals and prey to dictators to solve our problems. Don't be too quick to dismiss the possibility. It has already happened. They called it Nazi Germany — a strong government in a Christian nation that promised to solve its problems by eliminating the "problems" in society.

July 24: Our children pledge allegiance to the flag but not to the Constitution nor to the Bill of Rights. Interesting, isn't it?

July 25: The psalmist's warning is a dire one. We will not be judged on our "patriotism." We will be judged on our globalism. Who will pass, I wonder?

July 26: When "the workers of the world unite," it may well be at judgment day. It makes for an interesting scenario. I can't wait to hear what they'll say about whom when they don't have to worry about losing their jobs for saying it. How will U.S. industries manage when third world workers stand to evaluate their performance? And for that matter, how will all the "patriotic" citizens fare who support their country's labor practices in other countries? It makes for interesting Christian speculation.

July 27: It is no time to be "patriotic" when the defenseless of the country, of the world, are being sacrificed to the goals of the powerful. Easily said, until you ask the question: Am I one of the defenseless or one of the powerful?

July 28: "You're not supposed to be so blind with patriotism that you can't face reality," Malcolm X said.

"Wrong is wrong, no matter who does it or who says it." Funny how we don't like to hear the truth unless we like the messenger. And messengers who speak the truth are so seldom liked — all in the name of patriotism, of course. We always say it's because "they didn't do it right." We never say that it might be because "we didn't do it right."

July 29: Patriotism is not political, not military, not economic. Patriotism is that commitment that puts the nation in relationship to the world and the world in contact with the nation.

July 30: Beware the Fourth of July. It beguiles, seduces, and leads us to believe that having done right once, we need never fear not doing it again.

July 31: According to a "World Brief," published in newspapers around the world in May 1997, "the U.S. army conducted secret simulated germ-warfare tests in Winnipeg, Canada in 1953. . . . The Pentagon lied about the tests, telling the city's mayor it was testing a chemical fog that might protect Winnipeg in the event of a Russian nuclear attack." That means that many people in the United States collaborated in the attack. On an ally. In peacetime. Tell me again: Whatever happened to George Washington?

AUGUST

Psalm 68

*Guardian of the orphan,
defender of the widowed,
such is God, who gives
the lonely a home.*

I *was a very small child, about four years old, when it happened. Rain had beat against our house for the entire day. Sitting at our living room window, lost in the kind of rainy-day reveries common to an only child, and counting raindrops for hours, I saw him come out of the woods on the other side of the road. The boy was thin, bedraggled, dirty, and soaking wet. I watched him crouch under our porch steps while the day got darker and darker. He never moved. I shuddered at the sight of him and finally went to get my mother. I don't remember the rest of the details. I only remember him sitting at our kitchen table in my father's clothes, head down, his hands strung limp in his lap as my mother ladled more soup into his bowl and spread more jam on his bread. Then they came in uniforms and took him slowly away as I watched from the safety of distance. When he left, he hugged my mother. She put her arms around him and kissed him on the head. Who was this stranger who had usurped my mother's love? And why? I have never forgotten the scene.*

It doesn't take a lot of thinking to understand why qualities like honesty, self-control, devotion, and love are components of the spiritual life. But hospitality — the fine art of being nice to people? Why — of all things — hospitality? The question captures the imagination of the soul. Why is it that one of the oldest spiritual documents in Western civilization, the Rule of Benedict, says hardly a word about asceticism but speaks over and over again about hospitality and the reception of guests? It's a conundrum that teases us with an insight worth having.

The answer, I think, is that hospitality is basic. It's what teaches us about all the other things in life. It's what prepares us to deal with all the other things. It's hospitality that teaches us honesty and self-control, devotion and love, openness and trust. The way of hospitality is more difficult — and more meaningful — than any asceticism we could devise for ourselves.

Desert monastics, spiritual seekers who went into the backwaters of Egypt and the Middle East to live a life of solitude and prayer, broke every rule they lived by on behalf of hospitality because to allow a person to wander through a desert without water and without help is, in the final analysis, to condemn that person to death. Hospitality is the fine art of having an open soul and a listening mind in a world where, alone, we would all die from starvation of the soul.

August 1: Hospitality is not simply a matter of opening the door; it is a matter of opening the heart.

August 2: When we reach out to the one in isolation and pain, we assure our own rescue when we ourselves are lost.

August 3: In a society of strangers that is based on fear instead of family, hospitality is more important than ever. It does not assume reckless disregard for personal safety but it does assume accountability for the needs of the other. Of course we lock windows at night and buy good screen doors. That's only common sense. What is important is that we don't lock out the good, the needy, and the lost with the dangerous.

August 4: Be careful not to confuse hospitality with propriety. What we do to impress the people we are required to impress is not hospitality. That's socializing. Hospitality is when I turn my space into safe space for those who come to me wounded by life, endangered by people, abandoned by family.

August 5: "Receive the guest as Christ," the sixth-century Rule of Benedict instructs the monastic. A loose translation may well be, "Receive the guest as the one who comes to convert you, stretch you, save you from yourself."

August 6: Hospitality is not a social exercise; it is a Christian virtue that is one of the few tangible opportunities we ever get to demonstrate "See how they love one another."

August 7: It's so easy to be nice to neighbors. It's when people come into the neighborhood that we've never seen before — the African-American who's taking a walk; the Muslim who's looking at the houses; the bag lady wandering through town — that the human heart is taxed to the ultimate. If we are "gracious and courteous to strangers," Francis Bacon wrote, it shows that we are "citizens of the world."

August 8: To be brokenhearted about the refugees we see on television, the children down the street who never see a parent all day long, the old woman who lives behind locks and blinds — and to do something about it — now that is hospitality.

August 9: Scripture is a catalog of messages from God that come through strangers. One scripture story after another details the blessings that come in the unexpected. The thought gives a person pause. Could it be that every stranger turned away is a divine message missed?

August 10: Max Beerbohm writes, "When hospitality becomes an art, it loses its very soul." And we do too. And so do those who play this game of substituting protocol for presence to the person of the other.

August 11: Hospitality is the ability to make another person comfortable in strange space: ours. Not easy, is it? Especially when that person leaves glasses in the sink and fingerprints on the coffee table. Then there's nothing left but the possibility of conversion, including ours.

August 12: Some people never hear a knock on the door from one month to another. If you're someone who feels that you hear far too many of them, instead of cringing when the door opens, bless your inconveniences. There may come a time when they are the only dose of reality, the only chance at life, you ever get.

August 13: Think of the person you trust least, care for least, in life. Now, in your mind's eye, bring her into your space, offer her your food, sit in perfect silence, and let her talk. How do you feel about her now? Funny how talk changes things, isn't it?

August 14: The Dhammapada, a Buddhist scripture, says, "The way is not in the sky. The way is in the heart." Don't look outside yourself, in other words, for the rules and orders and checklists that will assure you of your sanctity. Look instead at the thoughts in your heart, look at the way you respond to others, look at the number of times you smile at the people you are not expected to smile at during the day, and you'll know without doubt exactly what is still missing in your spiritual life.

August 15: The Irish proverb teaches: "Live in such a way that when you die even the undertaker will miss you." Ah, such a loss that would be.

August 16: Just for one day try starting a conversation with a willingness to listen to the other person rather than the need to cut the person off with old answers. Open the doors of your mind and let the other in.

August 17: What's the first thought that goes through your mind when someone asks you something: why what that person wants won't work, or why it might? The two responses make the difference between the hospitable heart and the closed one. They are far more telling of our hospitality quotient than nodding to neighbors in the church parking lot.

August 18: "If you stop to be kind," Mary Webb wrote, "you must swerve often from your path." Yes, but imagine all the scenery you'll see on the way that you never would have otherwise, all the roads you'll take that you never knew existed, all the places you'll come to in life that you could otherwise have missed, all the people you'll meet whom you would never have seen had you hurried through life. Hospitality may take us where we would not go, perhaps, but always to our own great good.

August 19: The problem with hospitality is that it is such a bother. That's why it's such a blessing. Blessings are outpourings of God's love where we expect them least.

August 20: Hospitality has become very organized and very antiseptic in the United States today. We take into our lives only the friends we've made on the job, or the neighbors we know, or strangers that someone else can vouch for, but not the unknown other or the social outcast or the politically unacceptable foreigner. So is hospitality an impossible art for this time and this culture? On the contrary. It is the only social art we really need if we ourselves are to be whole people.

August 21: It is so easy to give clothes to the poor but refuse to honor the ones to whom we have given the goods. And besides that, it cleans out our closets. Surely it would be holier to throw the clothes away than to throw the people away to whom we give them.

August 22: I had a flat tire last month in a slum section of a large city. The black woman who came to the door to offer help also offered her phone, her food, and her chair for me to sit in while I waited for the tow truck. I couldn't help but wonder how many white people would have done the same for her.

August 23: "Those are beautiful pictures," I said, looking at one of those daguerreotype prints on the old black woman's wall as I sipped the lemonade she gave me in the heat of the day. "My family," she said simply. "They were slaves." Hospitality happens when we put down the hates in our heart and let the other into our lives.

August 24: When I let strange people and strange ideas into my heart, I am beginning to shape a new world. Hospitality of the heart could change U.S. domestic policies. Hospitality of the heart could make my world a world of potential friends rather than a world of probable enemies.

August 25: Real hospitality lies in bending some efforts to change things, to make a haven for the helpless, to be a voice for the voiceless.

August 26: Hospitality is the way we turn a prejudiced world around, one heart at a time.

August 27: Hospitality is the willingness to be interrupted and inconvenienced so that others can get on with their lives rather than simply protecting the tidiness of our own.

August 28: Hospitality is the art of giving what you have to everyone in sight. It is not a series of grand gestures at controlled times. It is not a finishing school activity. It is an act of the recklessly generous heart.

August 29: When we close others out of our lives, we close ourselves to the rest of life. We become prisoners of ourselves.

August 30: Hospitality is the virtue of interruptibility.

August 31: Hospitality is the capacity to take ourselves out of ourselves, to change our minds and soften our judgments. Hospitality makes of every stranger a potential friend. Now that is holiness.

SEPTEMBER

PSALM 23

*Though I walk in
the valley of darkness,
no evil do I fear.
Your rod and staff
comfort me.*

*W*hat shall we say about pain? Has it any value at all?

"Once upon a time," an old Hasidic tale teaches us, "the local Jewish congregation was very concerned that their rabbi disappeared into the forest every single Sabbath night. Was he chanting with angels? Was he praying with Elijah? Was he communing directly with God? So, after months of this, they finally sent the sexton to follow him who would report back to them on where he was going. Sure enough, the next Sabbath eve, the rabbi went through the woods, up a mountain path, over the crest of the mountain to a cottage. And there, the sexton could see through the window, lay an old gentile woman, wasting away and sick in her bed. The rabbi swept the floor, chopped the wood, lit the fire, made a large pot of stew, washed the bedclothes, and then left quickly in order to get back to the synagogue in time for morning services. The sexton, too, hurried back and arrived breathless. "Well," the congregation demanded to know, "Did our rabbi go up to heaven?" The sexton thought for a minute. "Oh, no, my friends," he said and smiled softly. "Our rabbi did not go up to heaven. Our rabbi went much higher than that."

There are some kinds of pain that cannot be taken away in life. Loss. Hurt. Rejection. Disability. Those

*who enter into the pain of another, however, know what
it is to talk about the love of a God who does not change
the circumstances that form us but walks through them
with us every step of the way.*

*Pain is that dimension of human life that calls us to
give — and to be able to receive — the sometimes awk-
ward, often incomplete, but always healing care that those
who simply sit with those who hurt forever bring.*

*The real question, come to think about it, is whether
the congregation kept their old rabbi or got themselves a
new one — for the sake of the faith, of course.*

*To go down into pain with another person breaks open
the heart of the God who looks among us always for the
face most like God's own.*

September 1: It is not so much the pain itself that matters. It is being left to bear it alone that breaks the spirit and dries out the soul.

September 2: Pain is instructive. It tells us when something must be changed before all our energy is spent avoiding what we cannot possibly endure.

September 3: Healing physical hurt takes time, care, and awareness of the implications of ignoring the condition. Healing an emotional pain also takes time, care, and awareness of the implications of ignoring the condition. Why is it that we have no trouble whatsoever attending to the one but insist on denying the other? That's easy: in the first case, we are the ones who shape the physical conditions under which we live. In the other case, the psychological condition changes us.

September 4: "Will you cure the people who come to you?" the disciple asked the Holy One. "Oh, people don't come to be cured," the Holy One answered. "They come for relief. A cure would require change and that's the last thing in the world they want."

September 5: Comfort is a small and tender thing. All it takes is regular presence, patient listening, and genuine concern. Maybe that's why there is so little of it in the world. It demands that we go out of ourselves to the other in ways that advantage us not a whit. In fact, comfort is a very expensive thing.

September 6: "Our prime purpose in this life is to help others. And, if you cannot help them, at least don't hurt them," the Dalai Lama Tenzin Gyatso says. True enough. But it is also true that sometimes not helping a person is hurting that person. When another person's life or heart, hope or future is at stake, there may be no such thing as passive virtue, no such thing as simply nodding in passing when the person we are passing is dying of thirst, out of a job, or the mother of culture-deprived children.

September 7: Disinterest is fast becoming the national charism. We see homelessness and pay no attention, watch violence and look away, legislate poverty for some and affluence for others and cheer the "justice" that drives such cruelty. The modern slogan has become: "Don't just do something. Sit there." Now that's painful.

September 8: Only a healthy body can heal itself. We have to stay in the best possible physical and emotional condition if we expect to be able to survive pain when it comes. And it will come.

September 9: Don't be afraid to let emotional pain into consciousness. That is the only way to identify and heal it. Otherwise it will come out as anger, depression, despair, or purposelessness. Embracing the pain — naming it and accepting it, ironically — is exactly what takes the teeth out of it.

September 10: Comfort is not the useless exercise of trying to talk people out of their pain: "Oh, that's not as bad as you think it is." "You're not really hurting." "Don't worry about it." The fact is that it *is* bad for me. I *do* hurt. I *am* worrying. If you really want to help, simply accept my situation lovingly and ask what you can do to help me through it. Just signal the fact that my pain has some kind of human worth. That will be comfort enough for a person whose pain feels like total human obliteration.

September 11: It's what we have lived through successfully in the past that makes us capable of the rest of life.

September 12: Robert Browning Hamilton wrote:
> I walked a mile with Pleasure,
> She chatted all the way,
> But left me none the wiser
> For all she had to say.

I walked a mile with Sorrow,
And ne'er a word said she,
But, oh, the things I learned from her
When Sorrow walked with me!

It is so often what we lose that grows us, not what we can have for the picking that makes us wise, makes us whole.

September 13: The pain we hold within us is the ground out of which we grow.

September 14: It is only what we hold most dear that can hurt us most deeply. Pain is the measure of the love.

September 15: Never traffic in false comfort. Life depends on learning to confront pain, not in denying it. Amy Lowell put it this way: "Even pain / Pricks to livelier living."

September 16: It isn't that any of us can take another person's pain away. But all of us can help to bear it.

September 17: When Jesus found his three best friends sleeping in the Garden of Gethsemane while he wrestled in his soul with a sense of betrayal and failure, his pain did not lie in the fact that they were not guarding him from his coming arrest. His pain lay in the fact that they didn't even know — or worse, that they didn't care — that he was in pain. Pain separates friends from companions. In the end that may be its best service to us all.

September 18: "The most massive characters," E. H. Chapin wrote, "are seared with scars." It's what we endure, not what we avoid, that toughens us.

September 19: Comfort and coercion are not synonyms. Giving people "advice" they can't take, putting pressure where there is enough pressure already is not comfort. Don't give advice unless asked. Be careful about giving directions. Just sit and help people sift through their options themselves. That is comfort. That is real care.

September 20: The God who walked with Moses, forgave David, chose Mary, and bore you in the womb of life is the very God who will sustain you too.

September 21: Pain is simply the signal that something is going awry in life. It is not a deprivation; it is a gift.

September 22: Counselors know that those who swallow a stone become a stone. There are pains so deeply hidden, even from ourselves, that it is almost impossible to tell where they're coming from. When I find myself becoming what others avoid and what I myself do not want to be, it is time to reach into my heart and find the thorn that lives there.

September 23: We all want comfort, the kind that came on a mother's breast. After childhood has done its work on us, no one gets carried like that. The only comfort we can hope for is the support we will need to cure ourselves.

September 24: The African proverb teaches: not to aid one in distress is to kill that person in your heart. There is no pain more painful than being refused comfort when pain comes.

September 25: Beware the friends who smile while you cry and then pretend they didn't notice. Only those who reverence your pain really reverence you.

September 26: It isn't difficult to survive pain. It is far more difficult to grow beyond it.

September 27: There are some pains that can never be healed because those who inflicted them have no desire to heal them. In that case, the only recourse is to build for yourself a new life around the hurt rather than allow the hurt to smother the rest of life.

September 28: It is better to talk pain to death than to ignore it, not because the talking is easy but because the talking is cathartic. When the pain dies from the weight of its own repetition and boredom, it will be time to go on to more interesting things without having to bear the weight of past pains in the midst of all the joys to come. And come they will.

September 29: Nomura Motoni wrote: "This is a world that cages all warblers with a beautiful voice." Remember that there is as much pain that comes from being successful as there is from failing.

September 30: "The lowest ebb is the turn of the tide," Henry Wadsworth Longfellow wrote. When something ends without explanation, without warning, without preparation, something new is already on the horizon. Grasp it. There is life.

OCTOBER

Psalm 37

Commit your life to God,
and justice will dawn for you.
Your integrity will shine
like the noonday sun.

*W*hen the man threw his wife down the front steps of the building, the people in the neighborhood explained that he was a "good man" who had "a drinking problem" and was "out of work" and "couldn't help himself" and she shouldn't "nag him." I listened unseen to the adults around me as they shrugged their shoulders and interpreted the world to one another. But even at the age of eleven, I knew they were wrong. He may have been good and out of work and frustrated and sick, but lots of people are. That gave him no right to hurt someone else, to wreak injustice on another, to lose his sense of self. The difference between this situation, I knew, and the situation of the other people on the block who were in equally bad straits, had nothing to do with the circumstances. It had to do with the way they had learned to approach life to begin with. Something was missing here. What was it?

As the years went by, I began to realize that growing up is not difficult. Maturing is, however. Growth is biological and for all intents and purposes happens by itself. Maturity, on the other hand, is emotional and takes effort, takes personal commitment.

Maturity implies that something has ripened in us. Something is ready. Something is finished developing.

Something has become everything of which it is capable. Down deep, in the quiet space inside ourselves, we know that when we're mature, we are not at the mercy of our environment. We respond to life; we don't react to it.

The psalmist names the qualities that constitute maturity: commitment, justice, integrity, and spirituality. The mature person lives grounded in God, meets responsibilities, gives the world what is its due and has the kind of self-knowledge that leads to growth till the day we die. Adults do not hurt other people to satisfy their emotional extremes and then make excuses for it.

October 1: To be adult is to have emotional balance, full human development, stability, productivity, and social control. When we're mature, life is an exercise in judgment, not a ride on the wild side. It is one thing when a baby screams in a supermarket; it is another thing entirely when an adult does it too.

October 2: To be an adult it is necessary to have a soul that is as trained as our bodies.

October 3: Sometimes we mistake temper tantrums for anger and anger for adulthood. Nothing could be further from the truth. Anger is not rage. The only thing that rage does is to express emotionally, and without control, what we refuse to deal with calmly, kindly, logically. Expressing something and resolving something are two different things.

October 4: To be an adult has something to do with being able to delay gratification. Foot stomping is not adult. It is simply adolescence delayed.

October 5: When I insist on having everything now, I leave no time for coming to realize that I usually don't need it at all.

October 6: Zora Neale Hurston wrote, "There are years that ask questions and years that answer." Adulthood is the period in which we find out that most of the questions now new to us are actually quite old ones and that most of the answers are unclear. Then we realize that this is exactly the way life is supposed to be. It is not the answers that count; it is the process of pursuing them that makes us what we become.

October 7: Life is not unique. We all suffer, love, change, strive, and die. What is unique is simply the way we each go about it. Some struggle all the way; others, the emotionally adult among us, learn to accept every turn in the road with grace and hope.

October 8: Children have short attention spans and want everything that they see. Adults are capable of choosing between equally alluring things and then attending to them all the way to the end.

October 9: When we know who we are — recognize the gifts we have and live comfortably with what we lack, develop what we are to the fullest and give up lusting after what we are not — we are adults. More than that, we are happy. Not until.

October 10: To be adult means to be able to take responsibility for the generations both before and after us. It is not adult to make money at the expense of our children's future. It is not adult to take care of ourselves and ignore the needs of those who prepared us to succeed. To be an adult is to pay our debts to the rest of the world.

October 11: What we have been given in life we are required to return even better than when we got it. Only children take with no regard for those from whom they receive with an air of entitlement rather than gratitude.

October 12: Being grounded in God has something to do with being an adult. It means coming to an awareness of our limitations, of our place in the universe, of our dependence on everything around us. Children see themselves as the center of the world. Adulthood requires realizing that we are not. When we reach out to the rest of the human race, giving what we can and receiving what we need, we become fuller beings in the consciousness of our smallness than we can ever be in our arrogance.

October 13: When we no longer equate justice with vengeance and forgiveness with vindication, we have reached the level of emotional maturity that changes a world gone mad with rivalry, force, and childish selfishness.

October 14: Adults are those who are so mindful of their own failings in life that they are eternally gentle with the failings and needs of others.

October 15: Integrity demands that the face we present to the world is a valid picture of the intentions and aspirations of our hearts. When we say one thing and live another, think one thing and say another, feel one way and respond another, we have yet to come to full development. We are still two people.

October 16: "Don't try to be a saint. It won't work," John Dufresene wrote. "Just try to be a human being. That's harder." It is so easy to put on airs. What is difficult is to be a spiritual adult who lives out of principle and a consciousness of God in life — not escaping in ritual, not hoping for visions, not hiding from the world but looking at life and all its questions squarely, doing something lovingly productive to resolve them and placing our hope in God. That is spiritual adulthood.

October 17: Don't think for a moment that things change as we get older. Things don't change at all; we change. That's what makes life easier as we go. When we manage to become adults, all the childish demands inside of us become mute and disappear because we refuse always to give in to them. When they do not, that is a sure sign that somewhere along the line we have ceased to grow.

October 18: Adulthood is not that period in life when we begin to put our ideals down. It is the moment we begin to understand the difference between real ideals and childish ones.

October 19: It is important to keep enlarging the circle of our lives so that we can be brought to see beyond the walls of our own class and race and gender and social systems. Then we come to see what is wanting yet if the human race is to finally become fully human. Then we begin to build what the world needs. Then we become adult.

October 20: Western culture has tied the definition of adulthood to the ability to achieve. So we spend our lives getting education or money or things or status. As a result we are inclined to forget the need for inner development. No wonder we dissolve in despair when the external structures on which we have built our lives collapse.

October 21: Growth is more spiritual than physical.

October 22: Every stage in life is the beginning of a new life task. When we are young, it is identity we seek. When we are older it is purpose. After that it is co-creation, our gift to the world. Eventually, it is the acknowledgment of our limitations. Finally, it is integration. It is coming to peace with all the decisions, all the mistakes that make up who and what we are. When we have completed all the stages successfully, then we are finally adults.

October 23: To be an adult is to finally have developed the capacity to pay attention to someone else's needs besides our own.

October 24: The adult is the person who can deal with change without losing emotional control.

October 25: "The first step," Galway Kinnell wrote, "shall be to lose the way." It's when life turns upside down, when we don't know where we're going but manage to live in darkness with as much quality as we once lived in the light that we have come to adulthood.

October 26: To be adult is not to be perfect; it is to be aware of what we yet need to do to become perfect.

October 27: To be an adult, we must come to understand that we are incomplete without a spiritual life — incomplete unless what we say we are is the same as what we want to be, incomplete without a sense of transcendent purpose, incomplete if we would wreak on others what we would not want for ourselves.

October 28: When we begin to understand that we are part of the human race, connected to every other thing in the universe, we have become adult.

October 29: Every stage of life is a learning process. We never ever really "get it all together."

October 30: What is important is that we develop the willingness to go on learning. It is when we fixate at earlier stages of development that we lose the fullness of adulthood.

October 31: "When I was ten," the wag wrote on the wall, "I worried about what my parents would think about me. When I was twenty, I worried about what my friends would think about me. When I was thirty, I worried about what my bosses would think about me. When I was forty, I worried about what my neighbors would think about me. It wasn't until I got to be fifty that I realized that no one thought about me at all."

NOVEMBER

PSALM 25

To you, O God,
I lift up my soul.
I trust in you...
relieve the distress
of my heart.

I *got a computer when they were still advertising* *them as "time-savers." Do you notice they don't do that anymore? The truth is that it doesn't take a rocket scientist to figure out that computers don't save time at all. They simply enable us to do things twice as fast as we could without them so that we can now do twice as much in the same amount of time. The pace of life is getting faster by the day.*

Everybody wants instant answers to everything. Patience is a spiritual artifact — like gargoyles on cathedrals and memorabilia at shrines. The notion of having to wait for something is a thing of the past in the West. Food is fast, communication is instant, human beings are shot through undergrounds and airports, people do six washings a day in machines timed to the minute, money drawn out of bank accounts in one country comes out of holes in the wall on the back streets of small villages in other countries in a matter of seconds. The little things of life, the things we used to take hours and days to do — the cooking, the shopping, the banking, the traveling from point to point, the visiting and human contacts — are speeding up to dizzying proportions. We are pushed from every direction to go faster, to do more, to think less. We rush from birth to death, from place to place, from natural conception to test tube cloning in record time, with little or no opportunity to integrate any of them into our souls, to evaluate them with our minds, to come to grips with the effect of one part of life on us before we are faced with the demands of the next.

The professionals call it "stress." The contemplatives call it a "lack of balance" in life. The social analyst Alvin Toffler called it "Future Shock," the inability to cope spiritually and psychologically with the increasing effects of technology on our daily lives.

How shall we possibly survive it all without breaking down, without quitting, without rejecting the very things we must most be concerned about in a rapidly changing world if humanity is to remain human at all?

The psalmist is clear: distress is relieved by right-mindedness. It is not so much how much we do that determines the degree of stress it brings. It is the attitude with which we do it that defines its effect on us. It is the spiritual reserve we bring to natural situations that determines the toll it takes to survive the passing of time gone mad.

November 1: Life can rush us only if we allow it to rush us. Every phone that rings does not have to be answered. If I am not "there" in a way that makes me really available to the person on the other end, I am not there. So why would I answer? It is precisely the moments I am not "there" that signal me that what I need right now is a consciousness of the central core of life, the God of space and silence whose presence in my life steadies and secures it.

November 2: "Acquire inner peace and a multitude will find their salvation near you," St. Seraphim wrote. We can choose either to add to the flurry of life or we can, by our own calm, calm things down around us. People need the serenity that other people bring to enhance the quality of their own lives.

November 3: If you want to slow the pace of your own life and get back to normal, simply estimate how long it will take you to complete everything on the day's work list — everything: the mail, the drive into town, the bath, the meals, the meetings. Then double the time you estimated it would take to do it all and eliminate from the list what can be done later. That way, things should come out just about right.

November 4: Stress strengthens us, it's true, but it also chastens us. We learn that what we survive we do not survive alone.

November 5: Life's great efforts always call us beyond where we are to what we can yet come to be.

November 6: The problem with stress is that having too little of it leaves us emotional marshmallows, and having too much of it leaves us mentally and physically exhausted. The right amount of stress is whatever it takes to make us stretch ourselves beyond our comfort zone without leaving us with little or no comfort at all.

November 7: "Calmness," Ralph Waldo Emerson wrote, "is always Godlike." Why? Because when we can resist getting hysterical over passing things it is always a witness to faith in greater things.

November 8: It is hard to know which is worse: too much stress or too little stress. People often survive too much stress; they commonly deteriorate under too little.

November 9: Stress and distress are not the same thing. Stress is challenge that hones us. Distress is what happens when we pay too much attention to too meaningless a thing.

November 10: A Yugoslav proverb teaches: what is impossible to change is best to forget. But we don't. Instead we concentrate all our energies on it and wonder how it is that we don't enjoy the rest of life the way we ought to.

November 11: Stress is the process of paying undue attention to unreasonable demands for unacceptable periods of time. Whatever is the main work of your life must be forgotten at least half the day or it will sap whatever energy it deserves from you and will shorten your life as well.

November 12: For a good reason, we all can make an inhuman effort for short periods of time — and probably should — if life is to be filled with bursts of achievement. None of us can make abnormal effort over long periods of time — and probably shouldn't — if we want to live life with sparks and fire rather than turn it to ice and cement.

November 13: "The sun will set without thine assistance," the Talmud teaches. So why do we keep clocking it?

November 14: Some things cannot be rushed. They come only in God's good time. The important thing is what we do while we're waiting. We can push and push and insist and insist and flail and flail. Or we can state our truth and go on living. Again and again. Choose.

November 15: Pressure is when someone else demands of us what we know we cannot do. Stress is when we expect it of ourselves as well.

November 16: When we never give ourselves the permission to stop doing one thing in order to enjoy another, that's stress. It is not only unhealthy; it is unworthy of the gift of life.

November 17: I saw a woman walking a very young golden retriever down the main street of an Australian city. The little dog had a bright yellow blanket on him, the sign on which read in large letters: GUIDE DOG PUPPY. Now that, I thought, looking at the little guy and his twitching nose, is stress. Try not to set your heart on unreal goals. Who knows? You may be lucky enough not to make them.

November 18: Stress is what comes when we are taxed to do even better than we have in the past. Distress comes when we are taxed beyond our power to endure. Stress in proper proportions is a positive part of life, and God is present in it calling us on.

November 19: A life without stress is a life without challenge. That's not only dull; that's deadening.

November 20: It isn't life without stress we need. It is life with a large enough repertoire of coping skills to enable us to meet our next challenge. What we really need are the spiritual, communal, and intellectual supports to best the worst of them.

November 21: Denial, self-medication, and pessimism are not the answer to stress. On the contrary, they only compound it. Too much of these and what was once a passing problem becomes a way of life.

November 22: The God who sees our struggle is the God who walks the way with us as we wrestle it to the ground. We are never alone in times of stress — we are simply called to recognize the mystery in it.

November 23: "Time and patience will turn the mulberry leaf into silk," an Eastern proverb reminds us. Don't be so sure that what you think you have failed at has really been lost. Most of life's greatest inventions have been invented at least twice before anyone saw the value of them. Arthur Conan Doyle, for instance, invented the bulletproof vest in the middle of World War I, but British generals refused the design because they said that "only cowards would wear them."

November 24: Stress can destroy us only when we think that there is no future but this one, no spirit beyond ours, nothing to do but whatever we are doing now in life. That is not pressure. That is the terminal disease of nearsightedness.

November 25: "It is well to lie fallow for a while," Martin Tupper wrote. Fallowness, in fact, may be the virtue of the twenty-first century. Imagine what the graces to glide could bring to a world in a tailspin.

November 26: Teresa of Avila prayed: "Let nothing disturb thee, nothing affright thee; all things are passing; God never changeth." People with a spiritual life, psychologists tell us, bear stress better than people for whom God is a question rather than an answer. Who knows? Maybe our stress level is the measure of our spiritual life.

November 27: The mystic Julian of Norwich wrote, "Jesus did not say you will never have a rough passage, you will never be overstrained, you will never feel uncomfortable. But Jesus did say that you will never be overcome."

November 28: The Chinese say, "The one whose heart is not content is like a snake which tries to swallow an elephant." When we strive for things we cannot do and refuse to accept the fact that we cannot do them, we concoct a recipe for eternal unhappiness. Real serenity comes when we learn to grasp what is graspable in life, juice it to the bone — and then let the rest of life flow quietly away.

November 29: Perhaps one of life's most stressful conditions is the development of an intense commitment to avoid stress at all costs.

November 30: In the culture in which we live, it is not considered acceptable to endure the headache that comes from hours in the sun, to feel a little stiff after a full day's work, to lie awake and think at night, to be required to control our own emotional responses. But when that is the case, we miss a sense of our own limits, the healthy tiredness that comes from physical labor, the beauty of darkness and growth in self-control. We learn only half of ourselves. What a loss.

DECEMBER

PSALM 126

Truly, God
has worked
marvels for us!
It is cause
for rejoicing.

ork, play, and celebration are very different. Giving life over to work is easy. The culture is geared to it. We are educated with work in mind. We vacation on work schedules. We structure family life around the work day. We are, as a society, centered in work. We also, as a people, know how to play. As long as the game is structured we are very good at it, either as participants or as regular, seasonal spectators. What we do not do nearly as well as we work and play is to celebrate.

If anything, it is learning not to work and not to play that are difficult for us. Problem-solving is noble, we're taught, so work is rewarding. Play is competitive, we discover early in life, so games give us something to win. But celebration is something that has no product in mind, no trophy to garner. So why celebrate? What's the use in it?

Christmas is the answer to the question. The fact is that life is more than a trial and a test. It is also the awareness that God's presence is always pure gift in strange places. Celebration is about learning to recognize the gifts of life. That's the real gift of Christmas. Unless and until we can celebrate the gifts in which we are daily immersed but often oblivious of—the smell of fresh bread, the understanding of friends, the luxury of silence, the talents of our children, the goodness of our neighbors, the dignity of our lives — life escapes us. It is only living that we are about.

Jesus in a stable in a strange place at the wrong time seems to be no place to find God. But the angels, the shepherds, and the Magi all celebrated what they saw under what they saw. Celebration is a matter of seeing more in a thing than may, on a daily basis, be apparent — and saying so. It is about giving attention to things that, at one level, demand little attention at all in life, but without which we ourselves could never be whole, would never know God, would shrivel up and lose our souls.

Christmas gives us the gift of celebration, the gift of loose and lively joy, the gift of a healthy life.

December 1: The ability to stop and celebrate is the spiritual version of the gift of sight.

December 2: Enjoyment is of the mind. Celebration is of the body. That's when dance takes over and the soul begins to sing outside its box.

December 3: "I celebrate myself," the poet Walt Whitman wrote. The thought is so delicious it is almost obscene. Imagine the joy that would come with celebrating the self — our achievements, our experiences, our existence. Imagine what it would be like to look into the mirror and say, as God taught us, "That's good."

December 4: Celebration unfreezes the regular, the steady, the humdrum in life and turns it into revelation.

December 5: The purpose of life is not to institutionalize regularity and call it fidelity. The purpose of life is simply to celebrate it and call that fidelity.

December 6: We reserve celebration for certain days, moments, events in life. What we really need is a life full of celebratory moments.

December 7: The day that does not have moments of celebration is a day without an awareness of the gifts of God.

December 8: "Life is a verb," Charlotte Perkins Gilman wrote. Life is to be lived, not suffered. Life is to be enjoyed, not endured. Why do we act as if life is a noun — a thing — rather than an experience?

December 9: Lack of celebration in life is a sign of the lack of the contemplative dimension of life. Why? Because it is of the essence of the contemplative — the one who has come to see life as God sees life — to see the goodness of creation and to go wild with the joy of it.

December 10: We are never afraid to overwork. We are rarely reluctant to sacrifice. We are seldom concerned about the effects of unending stress. But we hate to take out time to celebrate. We call the dry endurance of the unbearable "sanctity." But what if it is really nothing more than spiritual sickness masking as sanctity. Take the risk: enjoy.

December 11: There's a theology of sacrifice that says that dancing is bad, drinking is bad, hemorrhoids are good. Aw, come on, tell the truth: down deep, alone in a room, do you really believe that?

December 12: "At Christmas play and make good cheer, / For Christmas comes but once a year," said Thomas Tusser. And that's true. But there are lots of good things in between. What are you doing about them?

December 13: Celebration brings us face-to-face with the God of creation. Now tell me again: How is it that the time you spend working is more important than the time you spend dancing your praise?

December 14: We know we're really celebrating rather than just appearing at the party when we can let go of our public face to become the best of our happy private selves.

December 15: If you want to be a real person, here's a tip: Don't go to any party this season just to be seen there. Go only to those parties where you can celebrate the season, the people, the time.

December 16: Real celebration doesn't require me to perform a social function. It simply releases me to enjoy.

December 17: "Come, O Wisdom," the church leads us to pray this last week before Christmas. Celebrate the wisdom figures in your life. They are proof that, given the right models, we can learn to survive anything.

December 18: "Come, O Sacred One of Israel," the church sings today. Celebrate the Jewish tradition and the prophets in your own life who call you to a commitment to the widows, the orphans, and the strangers among us.

December 19: "Come, O Flower of Jesse's Stem," the church reminds us to pray before Christmas. Celebrate the ancestors of Jesus who prepared the way for his coming and then celebrate, too, the people who have made our own lives possible: the ancestors who educated us, who protected us, who mentored us, who trained us in the spiritual life, and who, in their love for us, gave us a sense of ourselves.

December 20: "Come, O Key of David," we sing in anticipation of the birth of Jesus. Celebrate the Jesus who opens our eyes to lepers, our hearts to strangers, and our lives to truth. Celebrate, too, the people who think differently than we do. Openness, after all, is the key to human growth.

December 21: "Come, O Radiant Dawn," we plead as the memory of Incarnation fills us. The celebration of the God of Growth in our lives — those moments of insight in which life comes newly alive in me — helps us to recognize those moments when I begin to see differently, to live differently, to function differently. A new friend, a new work, a new idea are all "radiant dawns" in life that can enable me to become more than I ever dreamed I could.

December 22: "Come, O God of all the Nations," we remind ourselves to beg of God this final Christmas week. Every day it becomes more and more important to celebrate anything that makes us think beyond what it means to be an American in order to become a wild, loving Christian let loose in the world to pollute it with love.

December 23: "O come, O come, Emmanuel," we remember with passion today. We must, then, learn to celebrate the moments in life when Jesus appears to us incarnate in a loving friend, an important challenge, a hurt forgiven, a hurt survived, a moment of invitation that brought us to new life.

December 24: "Joy," Leon Bloy wrote, "is the infallible sign of the presence of God in us." The infallible sign. Think about it. If I am not full of joy, I am not full of God. Or is it the opposite: if I am not full of God, I cannot possibly be full of joy.

December 25: Celebration is of the heart. It is not a party. It is not an event. It is the ability to see the wonders in life. To lack a spirit of celebration is to live with a set of blinders on the soul. To see a child in a manger is one thing; to see there the finest face of God that life has to offer — that is celebration.

December 26: Some people enjoy the center of a party where they can let themselves go in ways no normal day allows for them. That is release. It is a healthy escape from the straightjacket of expectation. Without release we are bottled volcanoes.

December 27: Some people enjoy the fringes of a party where they can simply allow themselves to be carried along on the energy of the group. That's renewal. It is a healthy excursion into vicarious abandon. Without the ability to be renewed by the gifts of others we are left to our own meager devices. How sad.

December 28: Without joy, life's daily darkness can consume us. The problem is that joy must be cultivated. We have to work at it.

December 29: We sit and wait for joy to come in life. We fail to realize that it is up to us to go out and create it.

December 30: Never be afraid to let go: an arthritic heart comes out of a rigid body. Sing a little louder, dance a little longer, play a little harder. Let life loose in you.

December 31: Once upon a time, two thieves were undergoing trial by ordeal. If they could walk a wire over the gorge, they would be considered innocent and spared. If, on the other hand, they did not cross the gorge successfully, the belief was that they had been "executed" by the gods for their guilt. On this particular day, the first thief reached the other side. The second thief, terrified, called to him across the chasm, "How did you do it?" And the first thief shouted back, "I don't know. All I know is that when I felt myself tottering to one side, I leaned to the other." Take a lesson: celebration is what enables us to lean to the left when life tilts us to the right. It's called, quite rightly, "balance." Happy New Year.

ALSO BY

JOAN CHITTISTER

THE PSALMS
Meditations for Every Day of the Year
"Chittister's Christianity is alive with spiritual radiance
that makes the ordinary gleam with light and meaning."
— *Values & Vision*

0-8245-1581-1; $ 12.95

SONG OF JOY
New Meditations on the Psalms for Every Day
"In the tradition of Pascal's *Pensées,* Merton's *Sentences* and
even *The Imitation of Christ,* Joan Chittister offers guidance
and inspiration a little bit at a time. A delightful book."
— *Praying*

0-8245-1661-3; $ 12.95

THE RULE OF BENEDICT
Insights for the Ages
Fresh insights from proven principles that chart the life of
many religious communities and that anyone wishing to live
a spiritual life will find useful.

0-8245-2503-5; $ 11.95

Please support your local bookstore, or call 1-800-395-0690.
For a free catalog, please write us at
THE CROSSROAD PUBLISHING COMPANY
370 LEXINGTON AVENUE, NEW YORK, NY 10017

We hope you enjoyed Light in the Darkness. *Thank you for reading it.*

crossroad

Welcome to...
The Monastic Way
by Joan D. Chittister, OSB

If you are a seeker of the sacred...
If spirituality is an important part of your life...
If you would like a daily companion along the way...

Subscribe to...

The Monastic Way

This monthly, single-page publication with daily reflections by one of today's most inspiring religious writers and speakers is ideal for:

- Personal daily reflection
- Homily starters
- Opening prayers for classes, meetings, group gatherings
- Faith sharing

$15 per year includes postage; add $3 for overseas mailing.

Send to *Benetvision,* 355 E. Ninth St., Erie, PA 16503 or call (814) 459-5994. Fax: (814) 459-8066

Quantity discounts available upon request.

ORDER FORM for The Monastic Way
Use this order form for your personal subscription or gift subscriptions.

Name of recipient _____

Address _____

City _____ State _____ ZIP_____

Phone (_____)_____

If gift, name of sender _____

❏ $15 is enclosed for each subscription ($12 subscription + $3 postage).
(Please add an extra $3.00 for overseas mailing.)

❏ Quantity discounts are available upon request.

Mail to: *Benetvision,* 355 East Ninth St., Erie, PA 16503-1107
Phone (814) 459-5994   Fax (814) 459-8066